# "...As I Hav[e...]

## Poems for Living and Loving

*To Emil Enjoy*
*God Bless*
*Ron Schlegel*

# Ronald Gene Schlegel

This book is dedicated to my Angel of Love and to my wife, Charlotte, who has shared with me some of the happiest years of my life.

Published and printed in the United States of America by:

The Purple Gorilla, LLC
393 Toilsome Hill Road
Fairfield, Connecticut 06825
Fax (203) 367-3459

Books published by The Purple Gorilla, LLC may be purchased at discounted rates for fund raising purposed and for volume orders. Write for quotes.

First Edition

ISBN 0-9661844-8-3

# Table of Contents

Ronald Gene Schlegel

# *Author's Note*

Throughout my life, I have been encouraged by some indescribable force to express my thoughts in a poetic manner. At first, I thought that it was heredity, some of which was probably attributable to my Aunt, Grace Lyon Benjamin, who was an internationally famous poet. I have included some of her poetry (written to my Mom over a 40-year period, and most of which I believe to be as yet unpublished).

It wasn't until later in life that I realized that I have been, and continue to be, guided by my Angel. This Angel, whom I have named my **Angel of Love**, was responsible for instructing me, in the middle of the night from my sleep, to marry my wife, Charlotte. This Angel also seems to have guided me in the type of poetry that I have written throughout my life.

As the result of this guidance, I have segregated the poems of this book into the categories that seem to best fit the general thought of the poems. God's love appears to be the overall glue that holds these thoughts together, hence the reason for the naming of my Angel, to whom, along with my wife, Charlotte, I have dedicated this book.

*Ron Schlegel*

1

# "....As I Have Loved You"

*"Whatsoever you do"* was said by Christ
    to guide us on our way.
*"To the least of my brethren"* defined with whom
    we were to live and play.
*"That you do"* defined our response
    to His holy request.
*"Unto me."* defined to whom
    we ultimately give our best.

For to *"Love one another"* is more than words
    that our Savior gave to us.
Its meaning is in our actions,
    in our daily chores and rush.
*"As I have loved you."*
    tells us just how much we are to give.
And with all these teachings as our guide,
    He taught us how to live.

# My Angel Prayer

**Angel of Love**, in me abide.
Through my life be by my side.
Guide me through the fires of life.
Help me in my times of strife.

Prop my ever failing heart,
and when I stop, push me to start.
Ever keep thy love in me,
so, in death, my Lord to see.

# A "Thank You" Prayer

Why can't I see you clearly,
For I love you like my own?
I know you've guided me through life,
And its many paths you've shown.

You've given me a loving heart,
And for this I am most grateful.
You've taught me how to give my love
And never to be hateful.

So, to you, my own dear Angel,
I pray you stay with me
Till I join our Father in Heaven
From earthly worries free.

# Living

Ronald Gene Schlegel

# *This Day*

Look to this day;
for it is life, the very life of life.
In its brief course lie all the varieties
and realities of your existence.
The bliss of growth, the glory of action,
the splendor of achievement.
For yesterday is but a dream
and tomorrow is only a whim,
but today well lived makes
yesterday a dream of happiness
and every tomorrow a vision of hope.
Look well, therefore, to this day!
Such is the salutation to the dawn.

*Kalidasa*
*(5th Century Indian playwright and poet)*

# *A Daily Prayer*

*Make a rule, and pray to God to help you keep it:*

*Never , if possible, to lie down at night without being able to say, "I have made one human being, at least, a little bit wiser, a little happier, or a little better off this day."*

*If you can put one torch of rosy sunshine into the life of any man, woman, or child, you shall have worked with God.*

# Moments in Time

Cherish today. It's a moment in time,
    Like the instant a poet finds the right word to rhyme.
We've not seen it before, nor never again.
    Time slips away, like the ink of this pen.

Once gone, we'll soon forget the glorious sun,
    Unless we look and slow down our run.
For if we speed by the fresh blooming rose,
    We'll never know what God plants and grows.

These moments in time define how we live.
    Each one that is missed escapes through life's sieve.
Like castles of sand that the wind blows away,
    Once gone, life's form returns to beach grey.

The snowflake has form, like prisms, so nice,
    But once under foot, it's just part of the ice.
So let's not forget to cherish today.
    Forget being grumpy. Let's play.......Let's play!

## *Title*

To concentrate on title
    is ignorance and bliss.
If this reflects your goal in life,
    its meaning you'll surely miss.
For life isn't what they call you.
    It's what you do each day
that makes living meaningful,
    and to heaven will light the way.

Moses wasn't president,
    neither was our Lord.
Their lives were filled with giving,
    which in death was their reward.
They looked not for pomp and glory
    in all their daily deeds.
For seldom can one find glory
    caring for other's needs.

Now when your life is over
    and God asks the life you've led,
will He be more impressed that you're "President",
    or that some hungry you have fed?
Will He sit you at the table's head,
    where you've always been in your greed,
or will He not ask your presence at all,
    and, instead, ask someone in need?

## *Farewell to a Friend*

To say "farewell" is easy,
    for "farewell" is but a word.
To think "farewell" is harder,
    for then the heart is heard.

How does one relay
    the feelings of many years?
How then can one convey
    a farewell without some tears?

We've shared the common problem.
    We've shared the common care.
And now that you are leaving,
    there's one less with whom to share.

# A Purpose

When young, my life's ambition
　　　was conquering the farthest star,
climbing the highest mountain,
　　　traveling near and far.
I wanted to taste life's excitement
　　　and sail the seven seas,
soar the skies on the wings of man
　　　and be lifted by life's breeze.

As I've grown a little older,
　　　I have a new life's dream,
contributing to our way of life,
　　　helping to direct life's stream.
For conquering can be full of fun.
　　　It's exciting to stand out.
But I've slowly begun to realize
　　　that's not what life's all about.

For life must have a purpose,
      and I believe it is to give,
To make the world a better place
      for your fellow man to live.
to help your neighbor if you can,
      and direct him in God's way,
or build a better playground
      on which a child can play.


Each of us must search his mind
      to direct him on this quest,
as we're all a little different
      in what we each do best.
So while I have a breath of life,
      I resolve to do my best
to improve life on this planet
      Until I come to rest.

Ronald Gene Schlegel

"…As I Have Loved You."

# Loving

15

**Ronald Gene Schlegel**

# The Paradox

A laugh is but a bit of love,
    a thing good friends can share,
a magical moment from above,
    some stardust in the air.

A tear is very much akin.
    There is no great divide.
For like a coin that's in a spin,
    love lands on either side.

Ronald Gene Schlegel

# *The Grace of Love*

We thank Thee, Lord, for Thy Grace of love
    that binds and makes us one.
May it stay with us throughout our lives
    till we join Thee and Thy Son.

For with its power, we can overcome
    the problems that we'll face;
and with each other, side by side,
    our lives will share Thy Grace.

We know now, Lord, it was Thy Grace
    that helped us first to meet.
Please help us use this Grace with care
    to guide our minds and feet,

to help Thee, Father, tend Thy flocks
    and do Thy heavenly will,
to help us answer to Thy call
    and serve Thee with all our skill.

# To Charlotte

I see in you the love
    That I always longed to hold,
A love that lasts forever
    Even when we're very old,
A love that says "I love you"
    In a very special way,
A love that is my very breath
    When there's nothing more to say.

I thank the Lord I met you
    And you said "yes" to me.
I thank the Lord you gave me
    Grandchildren to hold upon my knee.
I realize that God has blessed me
    With a family from above,
A family to call my very own -
    A family full of love.

# *Reaching Out*

When I reach out, Lord, and give them food,
    I know that You are there.
When I touch their hands to comfort them,
    I feel Your loving stare.
When I tell a little story
    that wipes away some tears,
that makes them laugh, or gives them strength,
    or soothes their inner fears.

When I look to Thee, I hear Your voice
    telling me You care,
and that by my side You'll always be.
    If I look, I'll find You there.
You give me inner strength, Lord,
    to seek and do Thy will,
to help someone who is in need,
    and help him climb life's hill.

For in this world, so full of need,
    You've blessed us with so much
that we can use to do Thy will,
    and give a "helping crutch."
It is by this act of reaching out
    that we so shine Your light,
that we can serve our calling
    and fight the heavenly fight.

# *Friendship*

The ties that bind are but a few,
    though called by many names --
A "good old friend," a "pal so true,
    who won't play any games."
But, in the end, there is one thing
    that's part of these above.
It's the gift from God, whose praise we sing.
    It's His heavenly gift of love.

# The Search

How many times have we heard it said
    that "Life today proves God is dead."
"The wars, the pestilence, and the rest
    even affect earth's very best."

"Why," they say, "if God is near,
    does death occur to those most dear?"
"Why does the world have so many poor
    who don't seem to be heard when they ask for more?"

To these, I say, "Your questions are just.
    Doubt the Almighty if you must.
But explain to me, if you can,
    a few simple questions of how life began.

If the breath of life doesn't come from Him,
    tell me, please, how does life begin?
The wind, the acorn, the ear of corn,
    were they always here, or how were they born?"

If we only believed what we could see,
    what a shallow existence our life would be.
For God's all around us if we just look.
    We must pass the cover to read life's book.

# A Way of Life

Don't ask this day for your daily bread
      until you have earned the right.
Do you love your Lord and Savior
      with all your strength and might?
Do you give yourself to Jesus
      each hour of the day?
And when His graces shine on you,
      do you bow your head and pray?
Do you love your neighbor as yourself
      and treat him as your own?
Or, do you shun him, 'cause he's different,
      and, yourself, cast the stone?
For it is through love and understanding
      that we communicate with Him,
that will gain us His forgiveness
      and deliverance from sin.
When we have learned to turn our cheek,
      and welcome the prodigal son,
Then, we will have earned the right,
      and, truly, **"Thy will be done."**

23

# *Peace*

What makes peace, a larger stick,
    or a larger piece of land;
a bigger bomb, or the assurity
    that you have the upper hand?
If you take away man's freedom
    and lock him in a cell,
won't your temporary peace of mind
    soon be a living Hell?

For peace is not an item
    that can be forced upon man.
Peace must first be born of love,
    pure as when life began.
From love grows understanding,
    and consideration, too,
which soon builds into a lasting peace
    when you have a trusting view.

Too many learn at an early age,
    "Do, before it's done unto you."
Instead of as our Savior taught,
    **"Do, as you would have others do."**
Jesus greeted friend and foe with
    **"Peace be unto you."**
If man could only learn to love,
    He would, in time, say this too.

# *Love*

See how young lovers bustle
      with the glow of their new love.
Their actions show a unity
      like the fingers of a glove.
There is no doubt about it.
      They love each other so,
that, even to total strangers
      their feelings surely show.

As lovers age together,
      this bustle less clearly shows.
Their unity of words and deeds
      takes on more inner glows.
They need not tell the stranger
      how much their hearts are entwined.
A soft spoken word, a tender deed
      will tell the observant mind.

For love is like a flower
      that quivers in the morn
to open up its petals
      when to the world it's born.
But, once open to the sky,
      it need not move around
to show the world its beauty,
      till its petals hit the ground.

# Trials of Life

As we face the many trials of life
       And dark clouds loom above,
We should think of God's only son
       And His message of **Peace and Love**.
For with these thoughts, we can bear the pain
       Of whatever we must face.
And with His love, we can live our lives
       Knowing we share His grace.

God gave His son to die for us
       And help us with our strife,
To help us with our daily cares
       And to live a loving life.
"Peace" is what He said to those
       Who challenged His very way.
Peace will give the inner love
       We need to face each day.

But how do we start down this path
    With our lives so full of grief?
We can hardly think of inner peace
    When we're crying for some relief.
**Prayer**, my friends, is the answer.
    For He listens to our every thought.
He will always answer our callings
    Even when we're terribly wrought.

We may not always understand
    The directions that we hear.
But listen hard and we will see
    The course that we must steer.
His thoughts will be in our minds,
    But we must be willing to listen.
And when we open our hearts to Him,
    Our lives will start to glisten.

## A Feeling Heart

The cure for what "ills" the world today
is not an overstuffed head.
Man and his mind make a cold combine
for helping, when all is said.
Kindness, charity, love - - these three
are needed so sadly today.
Give us, oh God, a feeling heart
to ease other men on their way.

GLB

# *Virtues*

**Ronald Gene Schlegel**

# *Integrity*

Who we are is what we do
      and how we work and play.
For people judge our character
      by what we do each day.
If we lie and cheat a little,
      who will surely know?
It just might be our children,
      as they learn and grow!

Children learn by how we act
      and how we treat each other.
We show them by example
      how to treat their brother.
And if we want the family name
      to be carried on with pride,
We should live our lives accordingly,
      with **integrity** as our guide.

## *Patience*

Patience is a virtue
      that we'd all like to have.
And, in this world of hustle,
      we need it like a salve.
But how can we possess it
      if we can't slow our pace?
The way we live and work today
      is like we're in a race.

Our lives are one big blur.
      Colors meld into one.
We just can't see around us
      when we're always in a run.
We all need to slow our pace
      and learn to touch and smell
The flowers in the fields around us
      before time rings our bell.

Unless we discipline ourselves,
      we'll never get to know
That God has made a beautiful world
      in which He wants us to grow.
The beauty in the world around us,
      our sons and daughters too,
Are meant for us to appreciate.
      I've slowed down. How about you?

# *Caring*

Caring is a way of life.
>It's always being there.

It's giving from the heart
>when with one's own love we share.

It's being like our Lord
>when for His flock we tend.

It's living the Christian message
>When the needy we befriend.

# Conviction

Conviction is an inner strength
  to direct and light our way.
It's that thought that signals right from wrong
  in what we do each day.
It's an automatic feeling
  that helps us live our life,
when the answer isn't black or white,
  or when thought is mixed with strife.

Many times our thought is unconscious.
  We're not sure the reason why
we do what we feel we ought to do,
  when on instinct we rely.
When decisions can be thought out,
  we have a guiding light:
God's commandments of love to show the way
  and be sure our decisions are right.

All of God's laws are based on love.
  This one point Jesus stressed.
So, if we live our lives as Jesus would,
  His example will show our best.
We can be sure that our convictions
  are, then, guided from above,
if we make our decisions accordingly,
  basing them on love.

# *Planning*

If we don't plan thoughtfully for tomorrow,
we shouldn't complain today about those things
over which we could have had some control;
for **today is but yesterday's tomorrow.**

# *Perfection*

The quest for perfection is noble, but one should beware, lest that which is sought take on the perception of reality.

Remember, only those not in the game never drop the ball.

"...As I Have Loved You."

# *Death*

37

Ronald Gene Schlegel

## Death's Consolation

Why does death hurt so much
to those who are left behind?
Because memories linger of fun times spent
and visions remain in our mind.
We wonder what life could have been
had God not been so swift
to remove a loved one from our midst
when life is such a gift.

Yet it's hard to know the reason why
that God has taken from us
a piece of our heart, our very soul,
with neither warning nor fuss.
Our consolation is in knowing
that God's Heavenly Kingdom awaits
those who have made their peace with Him.
For them, He opens His Gates.

Where hatred will be turned to love,
and all injuries will be pardoned.
Where doubt is gone and faith abounds
and peace replaces a heart hardened.
Where our darkness will be turned to light
and we will feel His peace.
So we can comfort in God's promise of life
knowing that death is but a release.

# A Close Encounter Prayer

I found the "needle" to pass through.
I pushed my "camel" till it was blue,
but found that this I could not do,
for I had not made my peace with You.

So to You, My Lord, I ask not to die,
so I should live, and again might try
to live a life whose actions cry,
"On Thee, Dear Lord, let me rely."

My life, thus far, has been full of sin.
I need a new life to begin,
one that lets my heart open,
and to Thy flock be like their kin.

I know, My God, if my cry You hear,
that I can wipe away my tear,
and that in my heart I'll hold most dear
the thought that You'll be ever near.

# Epitaph of a Christian

Here I lie beneath this stone.
    In God, I put my trust.
I'm sure that I am not alone
    as my body turns to dust.
If He approved of my life on earth,
    and if I showed enough love,
then I am now in His Heavenly Berth,
    At peace, in Heaven above.

# *Eulogy*

She was a pretty lady,
    this worldly ship we knew.
She sailed so proudly on the seas
    and lofty sails she flew.
We always knew of her presence,
    for in silence she stood tall.
Whether sails unfurled or folded,
    her stature was seen by all.

She gracefully cut through the waves of life.
    She was never seen to complain;
for she seemed to enjoy the challenge
    of her tall masts at strain.
She brought so much pleasure
    to those she carried afar,
that, for her, life seemed as effortless
    as gazing at a star.

But now, this ship must leave us,
          for death has darkened her door.
We're saddened as she leaves our port
          to ere return no more.
Our joy, my friends, is in knowing
          that she's entering another port,
and the heavenly kingdom is welcoming her
          as she sails its celestial court.


Where seas are always calm,
          but where the wind always fills her sails,
where every day is a "number ten"
          with never any gales.
Where all of life's journeys
          have been tallied on "God's board,"
where she needs to log her time no more,
          for **she's sailing with our Lord.**

## *Eulogy* - 2

He was a stately clipper,
      this worldly ship we knew.
He sailed so proudly on the seas
      and lofty sails he flew.
We always knew of his presence,
      for in silence he stood tall.
Whether sails unfurled or folded,
      his stature was seen by all.

He gracefully cut through the waves of life.
      He was never seen to complain;
for he seemed to enjoy the challenge
      of his tall masts at strain.
He brought so much pleasure
      to those he carried afar,
that, for him, life seemed as effortless
      as gazing at a star.

But now, this ship must leave us,
      for death has darkened his door.
We're saddened as he leaves our port
      to ere return no more.
Our joy, my friends, is in knowing
      that he's entering another port,
and the heavenly kingdom is welcoming him
      as he sails its celestial court.


Where seas are always calm,
      but where the wind always fills his sails,
where every day is a "number ten"
      with never any gales.
Where all of life's journeys
      have been tallied on "God's board,"
where he needs to log his time no more,
      for **he's sailing with our Lord.**

# Farewell, Mom

## (From Your Three Sons)

We know our Lord is with you
      as you leave our earthly port,
and that His angels will guide you
      into His Heavenly Court.
We'll always share your memory,
      as you filled our lives with love,
and listen for your guidance
      as you direct us from above.

In life, you were our mentor.
      You kept in our hearts a song.
You even treated us with love
      when we went terribly wrong.
So although, dear Mom, we'll miss you,
      we'll make it through each day
knowing that you're still with us
      when we work and when we play.

# Farewell to a Friend

We shared the common problem.
    We fought the common foe.
We even won some battles,
    though many scars do show.
We laughed when times were good.
    We cried when times were bad.
We thought that we could lick the world,
    and many times, we had.

You were a noble comrade,
    with whom we shared our load.
You gave with every thing you had,
    and helped us walk life's road.
You treated us like family,
    and loved us as your own.
You taught us from your wisdom.
    From you, our paths were shown.

But now, dear friend, you've left us,
    from daily burdens free.
We know that you are with our Lord, and,
    with Him, you'll always be.
Our lives have been enriched
    by having been your friend.
We'll always share your memory
    from now until the end.

## *Jimmy Viner Farewell*

Today we lay to rest
    a pioneer of the sky,
a man, who through his lifetime,
    taught many how to fly,
a man, who from his birth in Kiev
    in nineteen hundred eight,
was destined to become in time
    among Aviation's "Greats".

While growing up, this young man's mind
    built up that special dream,
and, when the time to work arrived,
    he joined the "flying team".
From starting as a helper,
    the road was hard and long.
But, through work and ambition,
    he proved his virtues strong.

At Curtis Flying Service
    his life of flight was born.
Then, instructing for "Doc" Levy,
    paths through the sky were worn.
He's been known and loved throughout the
world
    by men who loved to fly.
Like Wilber, Orville and Igor too,
    he helped open up the sky.

As chief pilot for Sikorsky,
    Many "firsts" were his to do:
first to log one thousand hours
    in 'copters that he flew,
first to fly his uncle's ships,
    "51's" through "58's".
Speed records, rescues and daring feats
    proved to be his fate.

Yes, Jimmy Viner has blessed our lives
    by helping pave the way
to make the field of aviation grow
    to what it is today.
So to you, dear friend, we give our thanks
    and pray you God's good favor.
For in your life, you've left so much
    that fond memories we'll always savor.

49

Ronald Gene Schlegel

## *A Reason Why*

Whenever I pass this little church,
I always pay a visit.
So when, at last, I'm carried out,
the Lord won't ask, "Who is it?"

GLB

# *Christmas*

Ronald Gene Schlegel

# A Little Boy's Letter to Santa

Santa, Santa, look at me.
    I've been good, as good can be.
I brush my teeth 'most every night
    I do my school work 'till it's right.
I never lie to dear ol' mum.
    In school, I never chew any gum.
I love my teacher. I love my books.
    I think that girls have pretty looks.

I have one little problem, though.
    When Christmas comes, I want you to know.
I tell a little lie or two,
    like what I've just been telling you.
I know, dear Santa, that I've been bad.
    Please forgive the problems I've had.
For I really try to do what's right.
    So, please bring toys on Christmas night.

# The Meaning of Christmas

Jesus, our Savior, dear and holy,
      was born, this day, in a manger lowly.
Toys He had not.  His life was meager.
      Teaching God's love, He was most eager.

"My Father loves the meek and the poor.
      To them, we should never shut our door."
"Love them as your own," He said.
      "Give them food and a bed for their head."

Christmas is a time for joy,
      when gifts we give every girl and boy.
But if we love all, the small and the tall,
      then we give Jesus the most precious gift of all.

# Poems by Grace Lyon Benjamin

No gift done
    makes Christmas.
No gift of light
    brings cheer.
But those with hearts
    that love us
make Christmas
    all the year.

GLB

---

May God send his gifts
    of Christmas cheer,
and love to bless you
    all the year.

GLB

---

Christmas is over.
    Are you glad,
or just a tiny wee bit sad?
    Hold the memory.
It's so sweet.
    Its afterglow is far too fleet.

GLB

# *My Prayer at Christmas*

Help me know joy,
that joy that comes to the world
in the person of the Christ Child
at Christmas.

Help me to see beauty,
and make beauty all around me;
to see it in the midst of gloom,
or in a snowflake falling.

Help me to hear Your voice,
to keep my mind open
to others' trouble or pain,
that I may aid in smoothing their way.

Help me to recognize Your plan
to help spread Your peace
and Your love to those in need,
of whatever creed or race.

Help me to share Your love,
that greatest gift of all,
given by You to the waiting world,
at Christmas.

GLB

# Christ's Birthday

All day long
      they looked for a place,
Mary, Joseph,
      but there was no space,
until at the inn,
      in a lowly stable,
Mary gave birth
      to our Lord.  No cable
to get the news out
      to a waiting world --
but a shining star,
      its light beams unfurled.
The Angels sang,
      "Peace on earth, good will,
for Christ is born."
      Oh, that we still
might see that star
      at Christmas time,
and hear the same story,
      as the Christmas bells chime!

GLB

# *A Merry Christmas on His Birthday*

Let's trim the tree at Christmas,
    with love and peace on earth.
Let's light the tree at Christmas
    to celebrate Christ's birth.
Let's sing the Christmas carols,
    with thankful hearts and gay,
remembering that Christmas
    is Jesus Christ's birthday.

GLB

# A Holy Christmas

If we'd make Christmas a holy day.
not merely a holiday,
with peace on earth, good will to men,
and time enough to pray,
then we might hear the angels sing,
"Our Lord is born today."
and all the world would join with us
in a Christ-like holiday.

GLB

Ronald Gene Schlegel

# 𝒜 Real Christmas

Christmas calls for giving.
　　　Find now, some girl or boy
who needs what you alone can give.
　　　Christmas calls for joy.
Spread happiness around.
　　　Forget your pain or sorrow.
Christmas calls for sharing.
　　　So, friend, go out and borrow
someone whose need is greater,
　　　far greater than your own.
Christmas is for remembering
　　　those people all alone.
Yes, Christmas calls for giving!
　　　To celebrate the day,
spread Christmas cheer around you.
　　　**THAT** is the **ONLY** way.

GLB

60

# Marriage and Family

Ronald Gene Schlegel

# A Wedding Prayer

*TRUST, CARING and SACRIFICE*,
    these words from God for you,
are rules to make your marriage work
    and keep your love ever true.

*TRUST* is always knowing
    your partner will do what's right
whenever a decision must be made,
    whether in or out of your sight.

*CARING* is always being there
    when your partner is in need.
It's always giving from the heart
    and never showing greed.

*SACRIFICE* means giving up
    some things you like to do
in favor of your partner's wants,
    and asking your partner's view.

If, in your life together,
    you keep these rules in mind,
God will bless you with His love
    and His peace you'll surely find.

# Marriage Caring

Marriage is like two flowers
    when they first come alive,
each needing liquid nourishment
    in order to survive.
As their only source of water
    is from their loving mate,
daily water they must never forget
    to have a happy fate.

Water is symbolic of love.
    It must flow in daily deeds.
In every waking hour
    you must care for each other's needs.
Never must you forget
    to fill your "watering can"
with love for each other daily,
    as full as when your marriage began.

## *Marriage Advice*

Marriage is like living
    on the USA's West Coast.
Sometimes the heat can burn you
    as tempers flare and roast.
In order to survive,
    on wounds, pour not the salt.
And, just like in California,
    never dwell upon a fault.

# A Father's Prayer

Dear God, I pray you bless
    my wife and children every day.
Keep them safe and healthy
    in your loving way.
Give them love and kindness
    for their fellow man,
and keep them all as free from sin
    as when their life began.

Give them wisdom to know the difference
    between what's right and wrong;
and, even though their days are troubled,
    keep in their hearts a song.
Please bless my children, Father,
    with a family such as mine,
and let their children's children
    grow in Thy faith divine.

# To Kenn and Pete, From Dad

To be your Dad, I'm proud,
     as proud as I can be.
To see how you've developed
     into fine young men (like me).
Your music is inspiring,
     your spirits, a delight.
Aren't you ashamed to have so much
     and still be so damned bright*?

# *Little Things*

*Little* words are the sweetest to hear;
*Little* charities fly farthest and stay longest on the wing;
*Little* lakes are the stillest;
*Little* hearts are the fullest, and
*Little* farms are the best tilled.
*Little* books are read the most, and
*Little* songs are the dearest loved.
And, when nature would make anything rare and
         beautiful,
She makes it *Little* :
      *Little* pearls,
      *Little* diamonds,
      *Little* dew drops.
Life is made up of *"Littles."*
Day is made up of *Little* beams,
And night is adorned with *Little* stars.
And we, this glorious Christmas, have been
Blessed with our *Little Hannah.*

# A Wandering Child

A child of Thine, Oh Lord,
      has wronged and gone astray.
He has wandered into temptation's folds
      and turned to dope this day.
Dear Lord, I pray with all my heart
      that Thy love will give the will
he needs to stave this, the Devil's food,
      before it starts to kill.

Ronald Gene Schlegel

## The Man of the House

Housework is a thing
    that men will fight about.
"I shouldn't have to clean the house,"
    you can hear them shout.
"Wives don't have to go to work
    and bring home the bacon.
When I get home, I want to rest,
    for my poor feet are aching."

Some men never realize
    that wives have hard jobs too:
taking care of little ones
    that stick to them like glue,
cleaning floors and windows,
    and cooking all the meals.
They never give a thought or two
    to just how "Wifey" feels.

But this man thinks it fair
    to share the daily chores,
to help with everything he can,
    and even clean the floors.
For marriage takes this sharing
    to make this union work.
And that means picking up the mop,
    and from housework, never shirk.

# Lugging

The final day of lugging
    for our children has arrived.
And I'm happy to report
    that Char and Ron survived.
We've cherished every moment.
    We've loved our chance to lug.
But now that they have passed,
    we'll have more time to hug!

Ronald Gene Schlegel

# 𝒜 Personal Prayer

*Lord, you know I am growing older.*

*Keep me from becoming talkative and possessed with the idea that I must express myself on every subject.*

*Release me from craving to straighten out everyone's affairs.*

*Keep me from the recital of endless detail. Give me the strength to get to the point.*

*Seal my lips when I am inclined to tell of my aches and pains. They are increasing with the passing years, and the love to speak of them grows sweeter as time goes by.*

*Teach me the glorious lesson that occasionally I may be wrong.*

*Make me thoughtful, but not nosy, helpful but not bossy.*

*With my vast store of wisdom and experiences, it does seem a pity not to use it at all, but You know, Lord, that I want a few friends in the end.*

*Amen*

*P.S., Give me the knowledge to know what is Right and the strength to Do It!*

*Walter J. Schlegel*

"...As I Have Loved You."

# Nature

Ronald Gene Schlegel

# Autumn in New England

Autumn is a time when the leaves turn red,
    and orange, and yellow, and brown.
The frost appears in the early morn
    and the leaves fall all over town.
I am sad to see the cold weather come
    and see the summer go.
But I soon forget my sadness
    at the first winter snow.

# The Character of Vermont

Bubbling brooks, shades of azure,
        a table for two in "The Den's" small stall.
Chilled filled nights, the Von Trapp Family Lodge,
        the character of Vermont in the Fall,
A weekend at Stratton, just made for two,
        this time a January delight.
What better way to rest one's soul,
        or send one's cares to flight?
For in **God's Playground** we find repose
        and freedom, with all its rest.
The mountains, the air, the friendly smile
        make Vermont the very best.

# Spring

Our icy pond has melted.
   The geese are flying North.
Their noisy "kronks" portend the change
   that Spring is bringing forth.
The Robins have returned.
   The Crocus is in bloom.
The buds of life are springing up.
   Mother Nature has begun her groom.
No need for Easter bonnets
   or flashing lights to say
that Spring has turned the corner,
   for I heard it come today.

Ronald Gene Schlegel

# My Kind of Town

The well of the Indian legend,
    the hills as white as snow,
the streets named after nut trees,
    whose leaves, in Fall, do blow,
a city full of history,
    a past, which old folks say
started with the Paugassett
    at the park where children play.

The city, my friends, is Shelton,
    a city full of love,
where many have raised their children,
    guided from above.
I've traveled the world over.
    I've seen the near and far.
But this is where I've made my bed,
    where my heart shines like a star.

My children have roamed its many woods.
　　　We've watched the city grow.
We've petted the cows at the Hudak farm.
　　　We've built snow men in the snow.
We've planted little seedlings,
　　　which were nothing but a twig.
Now many years have passed us by
　　　and these trees have grown so big.

This is where I want to be,
　　　where people show they care,
from the Plumb Memorial Library
　　　to a Huntington Christmas Fair.
For home is where the heart is,
　　　and I plan to make my quest
to help keep Shelton on the map
　　　as "ONE OF CONNECTICUT'S BEST".

Ronald Gene Schlegel

# Miscellaneous

Ronald Gene Schlegel

## *Thought for the Day*

As you wander on through life, brother,
whatever be your goal,
remember this simple message,
as it's healthy for the soul.
Its meaning is profound,
yet very short and curt.
"It don't make no never-mind
if it don't do no hurt."

## Right of Way

Here lies the body of Jonathan Gray,
    Who died while taking his right of way.
He was right--dead right--as he sped along,
    But he's just as dead as if he'd been wrong.

Anonymous

# Pass a Compliment

Compliments are easy.
They take so little time.
To say "thank you" or "a job well done"
doesn't even cost a dime!
So, why are we reluctant
to pass along some praise?
Are we really worried
that this might mean a raise?

If we pass this opportunity,
there's a golden moment lost
to motivate a worker
with very little cost.
So, if we seize the moment
to compliment someone,
frowns will turn to smiles
and work will seem like fun.

But more than this is gained;
For fun is "bottom line,"
when workers really like their jobs
and everything seems "fine."
So output is the winner
of this "Pass a Compliment" theme,
and we can all feel better
that our future will be our dream.

Ronald Gene Schlegel

# Happy 50th Birthday

Fifty is that time of life
      when "things" may start to go.
You may not notice "what" at first,
      for "things" fail mighty slow - -
the *limp* that others notice,
      the *twitch* that won't go 'way,
those ugly little *wrinkles*
      that say, "I'd like to stay."

But life past fifty ain't that bad,
      for now, *they'll call you "Sir."*
*Ladies may open the door for you,*
      though that might raise your fur.
Just think, that ten more years from now,
      *the shows will be "half price,"*
with *free coffee at McDonalds'!*
      Now, wouldn't that be nice?

# Happy 60th Birthday

We've come today to welcome you
    to a very prestigious club.
A club that has nobility,
    so, to thee, **"Old Fart,"** we dub.
A club that allows its members
    to snooze a little each day.
A club that lets you ignore the fact
    that you're slowly turning gray.

The rocking chair is its symbol,
    for it's one of the only sports
in which you can participate
    and not feel out of sorts.
The name of the club you may want to know
    so its symbol you can hang
in a place for all your friends to see;
    for it's the **"Over the Hill Gang."**

Welcome, today, it's all these honors
    on thee, we now bestow.
Your vests you can now let out.
    Those size thirty-two pants you can throw.
For **sixty** isn't a catastrophe,
    but just another hill
that once you've climbed, you can start to enjoy
    and feel its relaxing thrill.

Ronald Gene Schlegel

## Spirit of America

Since September eleventh, we've come to see
An enemy not well known.
But from embassy attacks and bombs at sea
His seeds were earlier sown.
This enemy hides beneath the rocks.
Our weakness he knows well.
With bombs and powder he sneaks around
And fear he tries to sell.

He failed to learn, however,
The "Spirit" of our land,
The love of God and Country
That's imbedded in our sand.
For we all stand together,
Trusting in our Lord.
We pray He stands beside us
As we answer with the sword.

The "Spirit of America"
    Is that of which I speak.
It's that which keeps us standing tall
    To those who think us weak.
Woe to those who think
    That they can beat our will,
For we stand by "Old Glory,"
    Its meaning with us still.

Our Democratic government,
    That lets us all live free,
Is a treasure that was dearly won
    For future generations to see.
So now is the time for us to say,
    "In God we put our trust,
To keep America the Beautiful,
    And we'll not fear some dust."

# *My Legacy to My Family and Friends*

To each of you, some of God's most beautiful people, I pass on a **LEGACY OF LOVE**. I have tried my whole life to live my life, as my Savior, Jesus Christ, would have wanted me to live it. I'm not sure how successful I have been at this <u>Game of Life</u>, but, I can say, with a clear conscience, that at least I tried. (Remember, as one author put it, "It is better to have tried and failed than to have never tried and succeeded".) I am giving each of you the ball in this Game of Life and naming each of you the quarterback for your respective teams. I am acting as your coach by giving you some of the rules governing this game, as I have learned them.

There is only one schedule to play and it lasts your whole life, but consists of only one game. It is a long game, with no time outs and no substitutions. You play the whole game – <u>all your life</u>.

You'll have a great backfield. You are calling the signals, but the other players in the backfield with you have a great reputation. They are named **Faith, Hope, Charity** and **Love**.

You'll work behind a truly powerful line. End-to-end, it consists of **Honesty, Loyalty, Devotion to Family, Devotion to Duty, Self-respect, Good Behavior, Serenity (To accept the things you cannot change), Courage (To change the things that you can)** and **Wisdom (To know the difference)**.

The goal posts are the Gates of Heaven.

God is the Referee and Sole Official. He makes all the rules and there is no appeal from them.

There are ten rules that govern the Game. You know them as the **Ten Commandments**.

Contained in these rules, there is one important Ground Rule. It is, **"As you would that men should do unto you, do you also to them likewise."** This translates into the **Legacy of Love**, which I hope that I leave each of you by the example I have tried to set in my life

**Love your family**, for, next to God, they are your first and most important responsibility.

**Love your work**, but in a way so that it does not significantly interfere with your first responsibility.

**Love your fellow workers and associates.** Treat them like your family and they soon will be part of your family, united under God by love.

Last, but not least, **love yourself**, and this love will radiate throughout your life in all your actions and will allow you to easily and naturally "win" in this Game of Life.

Here is the ball. It is your *immortal soul*. Hold onto it. Now, get in the Game and see what you can do with it.

**Ronald Gene Schlegel**

# Not for Sale

A Happy Ending never is for sale.
　　You make it or mar it as you live each day.
You weave a pattern, colorful or pale,
　　intricate or simple, choose your way.
You cannot buy it from a merchant's shelf.
　　It's won by perseverance.  Throw no dice.
To get it, you must earn it yourself,
　　and cherish it. For it is without price.

GLB

Ronald Gene Schlegel

# *Behind the Poems*

Ronald Gene Schlegel

There is a personal story or reflection behind each poem that I'd like to share with you.

## Author's Note

*"...As I Have Loved You"*

*This poem not only reflects what Christianity means to me, but I believe that our Savior's words also condense into two simple statements what He expects His followers to do with their daily lives.*

*My Angle Prayer*

*Some of us never get to realize that we receive constant guidance in one form or another from God. I believe that I am fortunate to not only have subconsciously received this guidance, but to have also heard one of God's angels, my Angel of Love, speak to me.*

*A "Thank You" Prayer*

*I pray that the rest of my life continue to be guided by my Angle of Love.*

## Living

Have you ever thought, "What will I do today?", "What is my goal in life?", or "What is really important?". This section includes some of my thoughts related to these questions.

Ronald Gene Schlegel

## This Day

*Kaladisa, an Indian playwright and poet, wrote poems of epic proportions for music and dance and is regarded as the most outstanding writer of classical Sanskrit. This poem seems to be an appropriate introduction to this section on living. It says to me that if there is something that needs to be done, today is as good a time as any to start doing it, rather than lamenting past inaction or spending all of our time planning for tomorrow.*

## A Daily Prayer

*These thoughts have been adapted from works by Charles Kingsley and George McDonald. Living these thoughts each day is my way of expressing God's message of love.*

## Moments in Time

*My life as an Engineering Manager seemed to be passing quickly. I spent more time at work and less time "stopping to smell the roses". The thoughts in this poem came to me one day while contemplating retirement and lamenting what work had caused me to miss in my life.*

## Title

*This poem was written after having dinner with two executives. The Vice President of Engineering for a major Aerospace Company was responsible for over 1,000 persons and many millions of dollars of programs. The President of a small privately owned company had only 2 or 3 employees. A comment was made during dinner by the latter that "If you haven't made it to President, you haven't succeeded in life". This poem is dedicated to* those "climbing the ladder of success". May they never forget the real meaning of life.

*Farewell to a Friend*
It was a difficult time in my life when one of my closest friends and work associate moved out of town. I felt his departure dearly.

*A Purpose*
These thoughts came to mind during one of the busier work-related times of my life. I was on a plane to Washington DC for one of many out-of-town business meetings. During this flight I realized that I had lead an exciting life but felt the need to concentrate more on giving something back for all the blessings in my life. I believe it to be important to establish one's goals and priorities early in one's life so that the real purpose of our existence not be over-shadowed by goals of lesser importance.

## Loving

Living God's message of love takes on many forms.

*The Paradox*
I have often wondered at how closely interrelated laughing and crying really are. As one learns through adversity, love is many times strengthened by a tear or two.

Ronald Gene Schlegel

*The Grace of Love*
This poem was written as a thank-you to God for my
wife, Charlotte, who was placed at my side by my Angel
of Love. Together, we have dedicated our lives to God.

*To Charlotte*
On my wife's birthday I thought an expression of my love
for her would be appropriate.

*Reaching Out*
I have always received more than I gave when helping
those in need. We should all go that extra mile when we
see something we can do to improve life. This poem was
written after spending time "reaching out" in a nursing
home. - - What a great feeling!!!

*Friendship*
True friends share God's love.

*The Search*
Deep faith is seldom based on superficial knowledge.
Faith generally deepens as one ages and lives many of
life's experiences. The "trick" is to recognize God's
presence.

*A Way of Life*
This poem was written after reading the great aviation
pioneer, Igor I. Sikorsky's views on the Lord's Prayer
expressed in his 1944 book entitled, "The Message of The
Lord's Prayer". These are the Author's thoughts for
living, guided by the Lord's Prayer.

*Peace*
*We sometimes wonder why true peace, based on God's love, is so difficult for mankind to achieve. We need to share God's love today in as many ways as possible.*

*Love*
*As lovers mature together, the character of their love changes, but the beauty of their love is not necessarily diminished. It merely takes on different forms of expression.*

*Trials of Life*
*This poem was given (I believe by my angel) to me one night in my sleep, and was immediately transcribed when I awoke. I believe God wanted me to share this message.*

*A Feeling Heart*
*A good thought for the day, written by my Aunt, Grace Lyon Benjamin. We seem to have had similar thoughts in our writing lives.*

## Virtues

Virtue is described as "A worthy practice or ideal". These poems related to virtues were inspired by events in my life.

*Integrity*
*A good example always teaches more than mere words can.*

*Patience*
*Although this was a later-in-life thought for me, it is a good one to be digested by many "Type A" people today.*

*Caring*
*This poem is dedicated to those who spend their lives looking after the needs of others.*

*Conviction*
*As I have taught my children, trust your intuition. God is always with you when you need Him, but you must be willing to listen.*

*Planning*
*Many times we are the victim of our own mismanagement.*

*Perfection*
*This was written to those who like to criticize from the sidelines but who never get their hands dirty.*

## Death

I started to think more seriously about death when the Super Constellation plane in which I was traveling was hit by lightning. The plane was out of control for a while and nearly crashed into the ground. It was then that I realized that I was not afraid to die. It was also then that I started to rely more on the Lord and dedicated the remainder of my life to His service.

*Death's Consolation*
This was written as a consolation to Bill and Wanda Snyder, after their son, Jim's, premature death.

*A Close Encounter Prayer*
For those who can, but seldom give to others, check Mathew, Chapter 19, Verse 24. One might then think these thoughts either after a close encounter with death or after realizing that their life is already in a close encounter with loosing the possibility of spending eternity with God.

*Epitaph of a Christian*
A gravestone thought for a loving Christian.

*Eulogy, and Eulogy-2*
These poems were written in loving memory of my mom, Dorothy Lyon Schlegel, my dad, Walter J. Schlegel, my mothers-in law, Dolores Webster and Lena Mills, The Reverend Charles Schwarz, my cousin, Robert DeVarney, one of my best friends, Bill Snyder, and my good friend and music mentor, Joseph DeCamillo, all of whom have passed into God's kingdom.

*Farewell, Mom*
After my mom died, I thought of all that she had given my brothers and myself during her life. This poem is, therefore, dedicated to her memory, with love, from her three sons, Walt, Ed and Ron.

Ronald Gene Schlegel

*Farewell to a Friend*
*Written in loving memory of Stan Labak, who worked with me for many years. A truer friend and family-loving man could not be found.*

*Jimmy Viner Farewell*
*This was written as a Eulogy to Jimmy Viner, who was Igor I. Sikorsky's chief pilot for many years and whom I knew and flew with while working for Sikorsky Aircraft. Jimmy was a nephew of Mr. Sikorsky who came over from Russia. He started working for Mr. Sikorsky as a mechanic when Mr. Sikorsky was designing and building fixed wing aircraft early in the twentieth century.*

*A Reason Why*
*A light thought by Aunt Grace, and one worth contemplating.*

## Christmas

Christmas, family, and holidays were always an important part of my Aunt Grace Lyon Benjamin's life. As such, she wrote about them often. I have therefore included some of what I believe to be her unpublished poems on Christmas. Enjoy.

*A little Boy's letter to Santa*
*A child's light-hearted view of Christmas.*

*The Meaning of Christmas*
A somewhat simplistic view of Christmas, with a loose, but meaningful, interpretation of biblical verse.

*Poems by Grace Byon Benjamin*
  *No Gift Done*
  *May God Send His Gifts*
  *Christmas is Over*
  *My Prayer at Christmas*
  *Christ's Birthday*
  *A Merry Christmas on His Birthday*
  *A Holy Christmas*
  *A Real Christmas*

I have always loved reading Aunt Grace's poetry. We seemed to have had a similar love for life and for our Lord and Savior, Jesus Christ's gifts to the world. She always kept a special place in her heart for family, friends, nature, and Christmas. I know the Lord is looking after her in heaven as she looks down on those she loved.

## Marriage and Family

A successful marriage takes constant attention and much hard work. I hope that these poems on marriage provide some inspiration and direction to couples starting on this important journey.

Ronald Gene Schlegel

*A Wedding Prayer*
These thoughts were inspired by the wedding sermon to
my good friends, Ahjaz and Shazia. I pray they live their
married lives accordingly. The sermon, based on advice
from the Koran, has also served me well.

*Marriage Caring*
This poem was inspired by another wedding sermon; this
time by a Catholic priest and friend, Monsignor Joseph
Fitzgerald.

*Marriage Advice*
Human beings, by their very nature, are imperfect.
Recognizing and accepting your partner's human frailties
is an important part of perpetuating a healthy marriage
relationship.

*A Father's Prayer*
I have always prayed for the well being of my family.
This Prayer reflects some of my thoughts.

*To Kenn and Pete, From Dad*
This poem was written to my two sons, Kenn and Pete.

*Little Things*
This poem was adapted from the poetic thoughts of an
anonymous author and is dedicated to our first
granddaughter, Hannah Elizabeth Haaijer, on her first
Christmas. She was born prematurely at 2 pounds, 3.5
ounces on September 7, 1997 and has since been a true
joy in our lives. With love, from Grampy and Grandma.

*A Wandering Child*
This prayer was written for a friend's son, whose life was being destroyed because of a dependency on dope.

*The Man of the House*
This poem is dedicated to all those hard working mothers who are not always appreciated as much as they should be. May their husbands follow some of the advice presented here.

*Lugging*
I wrote this poem after putting our four children through college and "lugging" bags, furniture, cloths, etc. back and forth for what seemed like an eternity. The boys were easy, but only God knows how girls can have so much "essential stuff".

*A Personal Prayer*
When my dad passed away, I found this prayer among his things. It was typed out on his old Smith Corona typewriter and signed. It expresses some profound thoughts that seem worthy of sharing.

**Nature**
This section is dedicated to all those who love New England.

Ronald Gene Schlegel

*Autumn in New England*
*I was lamenting one day on the change from a beautiful*
*autumn to a desolate-looking winter with its bare trees*
*when it started to snow. The snow dusting in the bare*
*trees then reminded me of the unique beauty that*
*winter also brings.*

*The Character of Vermont*
*My wife, Charlotte, first introduced me to Vermont and*
*its many beautiful features many years ago. This poem*
*was written after our first two visits. Since then, I have*
*become a true fan and lover of Vermont. A visit to*
*Vermont makes for a great and restful vacation, even for*
*a committed Connecticut resident like myself.*

*Spring*
*This poem was written after one of our early Spring*
*visits to a lake house in up-state Connecticut. It is in*
*loving memory of my poet Aunt, Grace Lyon Benjamin,*
*one of whose poems formed the basis and inspiration for*
*this poem.*

*My Kind of Town*
*When we heard that Shelton, Connecticut, was having a*
*Centennial Celebration and that one of its activities was*
*to be a poetry contest, my wife, Charlotte, suggested*
*that I should try to express my feelings for the city,*
*after having lived in Shelton all of my life. This poem is*
*the result of that challenge and won first prize. Truly,*
*home is where the heart is.*

## Miscellaneous

Some additional, hopefully thought-provoking, poetry.

*Thoughts for the Day*
This poem was inspired by the words of a gentleman farmer friend , Rudy Hudak, who, in his youth, used to espouse these words many years ago.

*Right of Way*
A good thought by an anonymous author for young drivers who are just starting to drive. My dad, who was a flying instructor well into his seventies, always taught me, "The right of way is something the other fellow gives you, and, if he doesn't give it to you, then you don't have it". The rules of the sky are very similar to the rules of the road.

*Pass a Compliment*
This poem is dedicated to those managers who seem to think that a "thank you" needs to be used very sparingly.

*Happy 50th Birthday*
At 50, things start to change.

*Happy 60th Birthday*
At 60, more things start to change.

Ronald Gene Schlegel

*Spirit of America*
This poem is dedicated to the memory of those who lost
their lives in the destruction of the World Trade Center
on 9/11/01. America will survive!!

*My Legacy to My Family and Friends*
I saw these thoughts many years ago from an unknown
author and they struck my heart. I decided to embellish
them with my own thoughts and pass them on to each of
you, with all of my love.

*Not for Sale*
Aunt Grace's thoughts seem like a fitting ending for this
book. So, go out and earn your own happy ending.
Peace and love be with you on your way.

# *First Lines*

Ronald Gene Schlegel